To those who have ever doubted themselves. This book
is for you.

May you find the courage to take the first step, the
resilience to keep going, and the confidence to realize
you were unstoppable all along.

With gratitude to the dreamers, doers, and
believers—you inspire the world.

Unstoppable

How to Crush Self-Doubt and Conquer Anything

By Taylor Morgan

Unstoppable: How to Crush Self-Doubt and Conquer Anything

This book is a work of nonfiction. While every effort has been made to ensure its accuracy, the author and publisher make no representations or warranties with respect to the accuracy, applicability, or completeness of the contents. The advice and strategies contained herein may not be suitable for your situation. Consult a professional where appropriate.

First Edition: 2024

Part I: The Roots of Self-Doubt

Chapter 1: Meet Your Inner Critic

The Voice You Hear, but Never Invited

If you're reading this, chances are you've already met your inner critic. You know the one—the voice that whispers when you're about to take a risk, "You're not ready for this," or sneers when you stumble, "What were you thinking?" It's the voice that feels so real it might as well be etched into your DNA. And yet, this voice isn't your friend, your guide, or even the real you. It's a squatter in the sanctuary of your mind, and it's time to evict it.

Before we do that, we need to understand it. The inner critic thrives on your lack of awareness. Its power lies in its ability to operate in the shadows, slipping past your defenses, disguising itself as wisdom, caution, or even care. But here's the truth: the inner critic is a liar. A clever one, yes, but a liar nonetheless.

To crush self-doubt, we first need to shine a light on the inner critic, understand where it comes from, and learn how to call it out when it speaks.

Self-Doubt: A Survival Instinct Gone Rogue

Self-doubt wasn't always your enemy. In fact, it was once your protector. Thousands of years ago, when humans were dodging predators and surviving in the wild, a little hesitation wasn't just helpful—it was life-saving. "Don't wander too far from the group." "Stay alert in unfamiliar territory." These instincts kept us alive.

But here's the problem: your brain hasn't updated its software. While the predators have largely disappeared, the warnings remain. Your mind treats every new challenge, every uncertain step, as though it's a life-or-death scenario. The inner critic is your brain's outdated security system, ringing alarms where no real threat exists.

Where Did This Voice Come From?

To understand your inner critic, we have to trace its roots. This voice didn't spring up overnight. It was planted and nurtured over time by three powerful forces: childhood experiences, societal expectations, and cultural influences.

1. Childhood Experiences

Think back to your earliest memories of failure or rejection. Maybe it was a teacher who said, "You'll never be good at math," or a parent who frowned when you brought home anything less than an A. Maybe it was a playground taunt, a lost game, or a moment when you felt small and unworthy. These experiences didn't just hurt—they left imprints.

Your young mind, eager to make sense of the world, interpreted these moments as truths. "If I'm not perfect, I'm not lovable." "If I fail, I'll be rejected." These beliefs became the seeds of your inner critic.

2. Societal Expectations

From the moment you could understand language, society began feeding you a script. "Be successful." "Be attractive." "Be extraordinary." These messages, plastered across billboards, movies, and social media, created an impossible standard. Your inner critic doesn't just echo these expectations—it amplifies them. It whispers, "If you can't be everything, you're nothing."

3. Cultural Influences

Different cultures shape the inner critic in unique ways. In some, it's tied to achievement: "You must be the best." In others, it's tied to conformity: "Don't stand out too much." Whatever the message, the result is the same—a voice that thrives on fear and keeps you small.

The Inner Critic's Favorite Tricks

The inner critic is a master manipulator. It uses subtle but devastating strategies to keep you in its grip. Here are a few of its favorite tricks:

- **Perfectionism**: It convinces you that if you can't do something perfectly, you shouldn't do it at all.
- **Catastrophizing**: It blows minor mistakes out of proportion, making every misstep feel like a disaster.
- **Comparison**: It holds up others' highlight reels and shames you for your behind-the-scenes struggles.

Sound familiar? That's because these tactics are universal. The inner critic may be personal, but its playbook is predictable.

Recognizing the Voice

Before you can confront your inner critic, you need to recognize it. This is where self-awareness becomes your greatest weapon. Start by paying attention to your internal dialogue. Write down the thoughts that surface when you're feeling doubtful or insecure. Don't censor yourself—just observe.

- What does the voice sound like?
- Does it remind you of anyone—a parent, a teacher, a bully?
- What are its favorite phrases?

Here's a powerful truth: The moment you name the inner critic, you begin to strip it of its power. It's no longer a shadowy force—it's just a voice. And voices can be silenced.

Exercise: Journaling Your Inner Critic

1. **Set the Stage**: Find a quiet space and a notebook. Title the page "The Voice in My Head."
2. **Listen In**: Think of a recent moment when you felt self-doubt. Write down every thought that crossed your mind. Don't judge or analyze—just document.
3. **Identify Patterns**: Look for recurring phrases or themes. Highlight anything that feels familiar.
4. **Name the Critic**: Give it a name, like "Doubtful Debbie" or "Critical Carl." Naming it creates distance, reminding you that this voice isn't you.

Reclaiming the Narrative

The inner critic will always have something to say. Its job is to chatter, to plant seeds of doubt. But you have a choice: Will you listen, or will you take back the microphone? Every time you challenge the critic, you reclaim a piece of your confidence.

This chapter isn't about silencing the voice forever—that's a lifelong journey. It's about taking the first step: understanding the critic, recognizing its patterns, and learning to push back. Remember, the critic isn't your master. It's just a voice. And you? You're unstoppable.

Chapter 2: The Paralysis of Perfectionism

Perfect or Nothing: The False Dilemma

"Why bother if it's not perfect?"

If you've ever thought this, you're not alone. Perfectionism is seductive. It disguises itself as a virtue, whispering promises of admiration, success, and acceptance. But here's the truth no one tells you: perfectionism is a thief. It doesn't just rob you of your time and peace—it steals opportunities before they even exist.

Perfectionism paralyzes you, convincing you that if you can't achieve flawless results, you shouldn't even try. And that's the real trap: perfectionism isn't about excellence—it's about fear. The fear of failure, the fear of judgment, the fear of not being enough.

The Perfectionism Trap

At first glance, perfectionism seems harmless. After all, striving for high standards sounds like a good thing, right? But perfectionism isn't the same as healthy ambition. Here's the critical difference:

- **Ambition** says, "Do your best and keep growing."
- **Perfectionism** says, "If it's not flawless, it's worthless."

This mindset doesn't lead to better results—it leads to procrastination, self-doubt, and burnout. Imagine a painter so obsessed with every brushstroke that they never finish the canvas. That's perfectionism in action: endless tweaking, constant second-guessing, and never feeling satisfied.

Why Perfectionism Feels Safe

Perfectionism offers the illusion of control. "If I get it perfect, no one can criticize me." But here's the irony: the pursuit of perfection often leads to inaction. The fear of getting it wrong stops you from starting at all.

Think about that project you've been avoiding. Maybe it's a dream you've shelved for years, a conversation you've been rehearsing in your head, or a skill you've wanted to learn but haven't tried. Perfectionism doesn't just delay these things—it builds a wall around them, making them feel impossible.

Signs You're Stuck in Perfectionism

Do any of these sound familiar?

- You procrastinate, waiting for the "perfect time" to start.
- You spend hours tweaking details that don't matter in the long run.
- You're hypercritical of your own work, even when others praise it.
- You avoid challenges because failure feels unbearable.
- You compare yourself to others and always fall short.

Perfectionism isn't a mindset—it's a prison. And the longer you stay in it, the harder it is to break free.

The Fear Beneath the Flawless Mask

Perfectionism is rarely about the pursuit of excellence. Beneath the surface, it's fueled by fear:

- **Fear of Failure**: If you don't try, you can't fail.
- **Fear of Judgment**: If it's perfect, no one can criticize you.
- **Fear of Vulnerability**: Imperfection feels like exposure, and exposure feels unsafe.

The truth is, perfectionism is a defense mechanism. It protects you from rejection, but at a cost. It keeps you safe, but it also keeps you stuck.

Setting "Good Enough" Goals

To escape the perfectionism trap, you need to shift your focus. The goal isn't to be perfect—it's to be good enough. That might sound counterintuitive, but "good enough" doesn't mean settling. It means making progress instead of chasing an impossible standard.

- **Start Small**: Break your goals into tiny, manageable steps. Progress is better than perfection.
- **Define Success**: Decide what "done" looks like before you start. Stick to it, even if you're tempted to keep tweaking.
- **Accept Imperfection**: Done is better than perfect. Every successful person has a trail of imperfect work behind them.

Embracing Imperfection as a Superpower

Imperfection isn't just inevitable—it's necessary. Think about your favorite songs, books, or art. Chances are, they're not perfect. They're raw, real, and human. That's what makes them resonate.

The same is true for you. People don't connect with perfection—they connect with authenticity. Every flaw, every mistake, every "not quite right" moment is part of your unique fingerprint on the world.

Exercise: The "Minimum Viable Action" Worksheet

Perfectionism loves to overcomplicate things. The best way to fight back is to simplify. The "Minimum Viable Action" exercise helps you take the smallest step forward, bypassing perfectionism entirely.

1. **Choose a Task**: Pick something you've been procrastinating on.
2. **Define the Simplest Step**: What's the absolute minimum you could do to move this forward? (For example, if it's writing a report, the minimum step might be drafting the first sentence.)
3. **Set a Timer**: Give yourself 10 minutes. Just 10. Start the task and see how far you get.
4. **Stop and Celebrate**: When the timer ends, stop. Celebrate the fact that you started. Progress is the goal.

Repeat this process daily. You'll be amazed at how much momentum builds when you stop striving for perfection and start focusing on movement.

Rewiring Your Mindset

Overcoming perfectionism is about rewiring your relationship with failure, success, and yourself. Here's what to remember:

- Failure isn't fatal. It's feedback.
- Progress matters more than polish.
- Imperfection is where growth lives.

The next time perfectionism whispers in your ear, ask yourself: "What's the worst that could happen if this isn't perfect?" Then, act anyway. Perfection isn't the price of success—it's the enemy of it.

Chapter 3: The Power of Limiting Beliefs

The Invisible Chains

You may not see them, but they're there. They've been there for as long as you can remember, holding you back, tugging at you whenever you try to step outside your comfort zone. They whisper in your ear, "That's not for you," "You'll never make it," or "People like you don't succeed." These invisible chains are your limiting beliefs.

Limiting beliefs are sneaky. They don't announce themselves like villains in a movie. Instead, they settle quietly in your subconscious, weaving themselves into your identity. But here's the truth: these beliefs aren't facts. They're stories. Stories you've been told, stories you've repeated, and stories you've accepted without question. And like any story, they can be rewritten.

This chapter is about uncovering those invisible chains, understanding where they came from, and learning how to break free.

What Are Limiting Beliefs?

A limiting belief is a thought or assumption you hold about yourself, others, or the world that restricts your potential. It's the mental equivalent of a ceiling—you can only rise so high before your belief system pulls you back down.

Here are some common examples:

- "I'm not smart enough to succeed."
- "I'll never have enough money."
- "People like me don't get opportunities."
- "I can't change because I've always been this way."

These beliefs are often so deeply ingrained that you mistake them for truths. But they're not. They're just interpretations of your experiences, shaped by your past.

Where Do Limiting Beliefs Come From?

To dismantle a belief, you need to understand its roots. Limiting beliefs don't appear out of nowhere. They're planted and nurtured by three powerful forces: family, culture, and personal experiences.

1. Family

Your family is your first and most influential teacher. Whether they meant to or not, the people who raised you shaped your beliefs about what's possible.

- A parent who said, "We're not the kind of people who get rich," planted the seed for financial self-doubt.
- A teacher who dismissed your abilities might have created the belief that you're not intelligent enough.

These messages, often repeated during your formative years, became the foundation of your self-image.

2. Culture

The culture you grow up in sets the parameters for what's "normal" and what's "possible."

- In some cultures, success might mean stability and conformity. In others, it might mean taking risks and standing out.
- Media, religion, and societal norms all play a role in shaping what you believe you're allowed to do or be.

The danger is that cultural beliefs, while widespread, can still be limiting. Just because "everyone says so" doesn't make it true.

3. Personal Experiences

Your experiences, especially failures and rejections, leave deep marks. If you failed a test as a child, you might believe you're "just bad at math." If you were rejected in love, you might believe you're "unworthy of a healthy relationship."

The human brain is wired to protect us from pain. Unfortunately, this means it often generalizes negative experiences into sweeping beliefs to keep us "safe."

Identifying Your Limiting Beliefs

The first step to breaking free is awareness. You can't change a belief you don't even realize you have. Here's how to start uncovering your hidden assumptions:

1. **Pay Attention to Self-Talk:**
   - When you face a challenge, what thoughts immediately come up?
   - Listen for statements like "I can't," "I'm not

good at," or "I always fail at."

2. **Examine Patterns:**
    - Are there areas in your life where you consistently feel stuck?
    - For example, do you always struggle with money, relationships, or confidence?
3. **Ask Why:**
    - For every limitation you identify, ask, "Why do I believe this?"
    - Keep digging. Often, the belief isn't about the surface issue but something deeper.

The Cost of Limiting Beliefs

Every time you accept a limiting belief, you give up a piece of your potential. Imagine a talented musician who never plays because they believe, "I'm not good enough." Or an aspiring entrepreneur who never starts because they think, "People like me can't succeed."

The cost isn't just external—it's internal. Limiting beliefs erode your confidence, dim your ambition, and shrink your vision for the future. They convince you to settle for less than you deserve.

But here's the good news: beliefs are not permanent. They're not written in stone—they're written in sand.

Rewriting Your Mental Scripts

Changing your beliefs isn't easy, but it's entirely possible. Here's the process to rewrite your mental scripts:

1. **Challenge the Belief**:
   - Ask yourself, "Is this belief true? Is it always true? Who says?"
   - Look for evidence that contradicts the belief. For example, if you believe, "I'm bad with money," find moments when you made smart financial decisions.
2. **Reframe the Narrative**:
   - Turn "I can't" into "I can, if..."
   - For example, instead of "I'm not smart enough to succeed," reframe it as "I can succeed if I keep learning and growing."
3. **Practice Affirmations**:
   - Replace limiting beliefs with empowering ones.
   - Write statements like "I am capable," "I deserve success," and "I am enough." Repeat them daily.
4. **Take Action**:
   - Action is the antidote to fear. Every time you take a step, no matter how small, you weaken the grip of limiting beliefs.

Exercise: Create Your Personal Belief Inventory

This exercise will help you uncover and challenge the beliefs holding you back.

1. **List Your Limiting Beliefs**:
   - Write down every belief that comes to mind

when you think about your abilities, opportunities, and worth.

2. **Find the Source**:
   - For each belief, ask, "Where did this come from?"
   - Was it a comment from a parent, a societal message, or a past failure?

3. **Rewrite the Belief**:
   - Replace each limiting belief with a positive, empowering statement.
   - For example, turn "I'm not good at public speaking" into "I can become a great speaker with practice."

4. **Take One Small Action**:
   - For each new belief, identify a small action you can take to reinforce it.
   - If your new belief is "I'm capable of learning new skills," try learning something small, like a new recipe or a simple DIY project.

Becoming the Author of Your Life

Your beliefs shape your reality. They dictate what you try, what you avoid, and what you achieve. The most powerful thing you can do is take control of those beliefs. You are not the prisoner of your past—you are the author of your future. And the pen is in your hands.

Part II: Crushing Self-Doubt

23

Chapter 4: Confidence as a Skill, Not a Trait

The Confidence Myth

What if I told you that confidence isn't something you're born with, but something you build?

Most people believe confidence is like eye color: you either have it, or you don't. They look at others who seem effortlessly self-assured and think, "I wish I were like that." But here's the truth: confidence isn't an innate trait. It's a skill—a muscle that grows stronger the more you use it.

The problem is, society has sold us a lie. We're told that confident people are special, gifted, or lucky. We're not told that every confident person you admire—athletes, entrepreneurs, artists, speakers—started exactly where you are: uncertain, nervous, and full of self-doubt.

Confidence isn't magic. It's mastery. And in this chapter, I'll show you how to build it step by step.

Why Confidence Feels Elusive

Confidence feels hard to achieve because we misunderstand it. We think confidence is the absence of fear, doubt, or hesitation. It's not. Confidence is taking action despite those feelings.

Imagine standing at the edge of a pool. The water looks cold, and you're not sure how deep it is. Confidence isn't magically knowing the water will feel perfect. Confidence is jumping in anyway, trusting you'll figure it out.

The first leap is always the hardest. But here's the thing: confidence grows through action, not thought. Every time you jump, you teach yourself that you're capable.

Debunking Confidence Myths

Let's start by breaking down some common myths about confidence:

1. **Myth: Confident People Never Feel Fear**
    Truth: Fear is normal. Confident people feel it too; they just don't let it stop them.
2. **Myth: Confidence Comes from Success**
    Truth: Confidence isn't the result of success—it's the cause. Taking small steps with courage leads to success, which reinforces confidence.
3. **Myth: Confidence Means Being Outgoing**
    Truth: Confidence looks different for everyone. It's not about being loud or extroverted—it's about being comfortable in your own skin.

Building Confidence Through Small Victories

Confidence doesn't come from big, dramatic leaps. It comes from small, consistent wins. Think of it like climbing a staircase: each step brings you closer to the top.

Here's the process:

1. **Start Small**
   Pick something manageable. If public speaking terrifies you, start by speaking up in a small meeting or practicing in front of a mirror.
2. **Celebrate Progress**
   Every time you take a step, acknowledge it. Confidence grows when you recognize your own achievements, no matter how small.
3. **Repeat**
   Repetition is the secret sauce. The more you do something, the less intimidating it becomes.

Real-Life Stories of Confidence Built Step by Step

Let me introduce you to a few people who prove that confidence is built, not born.

Story 1: Emma, the Reluctant Speaker

Emma used to freeze at the thought of public speaking. Her hands would sweat, her voice would shake, and she'd avoid it at all costs. But she made a commitment: she would say something in every team meeting, no matter how small. At first, it was just a sentence or two. Over time, she started sharing full ideas. Now, Emma runs workshops for her company, something she once thought impossible.

Story 2: David, the First-Time Runner

David hated running. He'd always believed he wasn't athletic. But one day, he decided to jog for just five minutes. It wasn't pretty, but he did it. The next day, he jogged for six minutes. A year later, David ran his first half-marathon.

Story 3: Mia, the Overthinker

Mia struggled with decision-making. She'd agonize over every choice, fearing she'd make the wrong one. To break the cycle, Mia started making quick, low-stakes decisions: what to eat for lunch, which book to read next. Each decision, no matter how small, taught her that she could trust herself.

These stories aren't about superhumans—they're about regular people who decided to start.

The Confidence Bank

Think of confidence as a bank account. Every time you take action, no matter how small, you make a deposit. Over time, those deposits add up, creating a reserve you can draw on when self-doubt strikes.

Here's how to start building your confidence bank:

1. **Track Your Wins**
   At the end of each day, write down three things you did that took courage. They don't have to be big—maybe you spoke up in a meeting, tried a new workout, or introduced yourself to someone new.
2. **Review Your Progress**
   At the end of each week, look back at your list. Notice

how your wins are adding up.

3. **Celebrate Yourself**

   Confidence grows when you acknowledge your efforts. Treat yourself to something meaningful when you reach milestones.

Exercise: Build Your Confidence Bank

1. **Set Up a Confidence Journal**:

   Get a notebook or use a note-taking app. Dedicate a section to tracking your wins.

2. **Start Small**:

   Each day, write down three things you did that required courage. For example:
   - "I asked my boss for feedback."
   - "I went to the gym even though I felt self-conscious."
   - "I tried cooking a new recipe."

3. **Reflect Weekly**:

   At the end of the week, review your entries. Notice patterns and progress.

4. **Set a Monthly Goal**:

   Choose one area of your life where you want to build confidence. Take at least one small step toward it each week.

Repetition Is the Key

Confidence isn't built in a day—it's built over time. Each small action reinforces the belief that you're capable. And as your confidence grows, so does your willingness to tackle bigger challenges.

Remember: confidence doesn't require you to have all the answers. It only requires you to take the next step.

Your Confidence Blueprint

By the end of this chapter, you should understand that confidence isn't reserved for the lucky few. It's available to everyone—including you. Confidence is the result of action, repetition, and self-recognition. It's a skill you can build, one step at a time.

Let this be your turning point. Start small, track your wins, and watch your confidence grow. You don't have to be fearless—you just have to start.

Chapter 5: Talk Back to Your Inner Critic

The Voice That Won't Stay Quiet

Your inner critic isn't just a quiet passenger—it's a constant backseat driver. Every step forward, every risk taken, it's there, second-guessing and sabotaging. "What if you fail?" "You're not good enough." "People will judge you." This voice, relentless and loud, thrives on one thing: your silence.

But what if you didn't stay silent? What if, instead of shrinking under its scrutiny, you turned around and talked back?

This chapter is about reclaiming the conversation. With the right tools and mindset, you can transform self-doubt into self-empowerment.

Understanding the Inner Critic's Game

The inner critic isn't a monster—it's a survival mechanism. It evolved to keep you safe by warning you of risks and dangers. But like an overzealous alarm system, it often goes off when there's no real threat.

Your inner critic uses predictable tactics to undermine you:

1. **Exaggeration**: "One mistake means you'll fail at everything."
2. **Generalization**: "You always mess up."
3. **Comparison**: "You're nowhere near as good as them."

Recognizing these patterns is the first step to silencing the critic. The second? Calling it out.

Cognitive Behavioral Techniques for Self-Talk

Cognitive behavioral therapy (CBT) offers powerful tools to dismantle negative self-talk. Here's how to use them:

1. **Catch the Thought:**
   Self-doubt often operates in the background. The moment you notice it, pause and label it: "That's my inner critic talking."
2. **Challenge the Thought:**
   Ask yourself, "Is this thought true? Is it helpful? What's the evidence for and against it?" For example:
   - Thought: "I'll never be good at this."
   - Rebuttal: "I've succeeded at new things before, and I can learn this too."
3. **Replace the Thought:**
   Swap the negative thought for a constructive one. Instead of "I can't do this," try "I'll figure this out step by step."

Reframing Self-Doubt with Humor, Curiosity, and Logic

Sometimes the best way to disarm the inner critic is not to fight it but to outsmart it.

1. Humor

Your inner critic loves to take itself seriously. Don't let it.

- Imagine your critic as a cartoon character, like a grumpy old man shaking his fist.
- Give it a silly nickname, like "Nagging Nancy" or "Pessimistic Pete."

Humor takes the sting out of criticism and reminds you not to give it too much power.

2. Curiosity

Approach self-doubt with the curiosity of a scientist.

- Instead of thinking, "I'm not good at this," ask, "Why do I feel this way? What could I try to improve?"
- Curiosity shifts your focus from fear to problem-solving.

3. Logic

The inner critic thrives on emotion, but logic is its kryptonite.

- When the critic says, "You'll fail," respond with, "Failure is how I learn. What's my next step?"
- Counter irrational thoughts with evidence and reason.

Scripts for Talking Back to Common Self-Doubt Triggers

Having pre-written responses can help you quickly shut down negative thoughts. Here are some examples:

Trigger 1: "I'm not good enough."

- Response: "I'm learning and growing every day. No one

starts as an expert."

Trigger 2: "I'll fail, so why try?"

- Response: "Failure is part of progress. I'll never succeed if I don't start."

Trigger 3: "People will judge me."

- Response: "People are too focused on their own lives to scrutinize mine. I'm doing this for me."

Trigger 4: "I'm too far behind to catch up."

- Response: "It's never too late to start. Progress is progress, no matter when it begins."

Exercise: Create Your Inner Critic Rebuttal Script

This exercise will help you personalize your responses to self-doubt.

1. **Identify Common Triggers**:
   Write down the situations or thoughts that typically activate your inner critic. For example:
   - "Starting a new project."
   - "Speaking up in meetings."
   - "Trying something outside my comfort zone."
2. **Write Counterarguments**:
   For each trigger, create a rebuttal. Use humor, curiosity, or logic to dismantle the doubt.

3. **Practice Your Script**:
   Say your rebuttals out loud in front of a mirror or record yourself. The more you practice, the easier it will be to silence your critic in real-time.
4. **Carry It with You**:
   Keep your script in a journal, on your phone, or on a sticky note. Refer to it whenever self-doubt strikes.

Why Talking Back Works

Talking back to your inner critic isn't about silencing it forever—that's impossible. It's about breaking its grip on your decisions. Every time you challenge self-doubt, you reinforce a new narrative: one of strength, resilience, and possibility.

Your inner critic is persistent, but so are you. And the more you practice, the less power it has.

Reclaiming the Conversation

By now, you've learned that your inner critic isn't invincible. It's just a voice. A voice you can question, challenge, and ultimately control. The goal isn't to eliminate the critic—it's to put it in its place.

From this moment on, the conversation changes. You're no longer a passive listener. You're the one with the microphone. And when self-doubt whispers, you'll know exactly what to say.

Chapter 6: Build Your Mental Armor

Why You Need Mental Armor

Life is unpredictable. Challenges, setbacks, and moments of doubt are inevitable. But the difference between those who crumble and those who rise isn't circumstance—it's resilience. Mental armor is the invisible shield that protects you from the world's uncertainties and empowers you to move forward, no matter what.

Building mental armor isn't about eliminating stress, fear, or failure—it's about creating tools to handle them. This chapter is your blueprint for fortifying your mind, so you can weather any storm with confidence and clarity.

Developing Mindfulness and Self-Awareness

1. The Power of Presence

Most of the chaos in your mind isn't about the present moment—it's about the past or the future. Regrets, worries, and what-ifs pull you away from the here and now. Mindfulness is the practice of anchoring yourself in the present.

When you're mindful, you notice your thoughts without judgment. You gain clarity, respond thoughtfully, and stay grounded even in stressful situations.

Practical Mindfulness Techniques:

- **The 5-5-5 Method**: Identify 5 things you see, hear, and feel in the moment.
- **Deep Breathing**: Inhale for 4 seconds, hold for 4 seconds, exhale for 4 seconds.
- **Body Scans**: Close your eyes and mentally scan your body from head to toe, noticing sensations.

2. Self-Awareness: The Mirror of Growth

Self-awareness is your ability to observe your thoughts, emotions, and behaviors without bias. It's the foundation of personal growth because you can't change what you don't understand.

To cultivate self-awareness:

- Journal daily to reflect on your emotions and decisions.
- Ask for feedback from trusted friends or mentors.
- Pause when triggered and ask, "Why do I feel this way?"

The Role of Positive Affirmations (and Why Some Fail)

1. Why Affirmations Work

Affirmations are powerful tools for rewiring your mind. When repeated consistently, they help replace limiting beliefs with empowering ones. For example:

- Limiting Belief: "I'm not good enough."
- Affirmation: "I am capable of achieving great things."

Affirmations work because your brain doesn't distinguish between real and imagined experiences. When you tell yourself a positive story often enough, your brain begins to believe it.

2. Why Affirmations Fail

Here's the catch: affirmations can backfire if they feel insincere or unrealistic. If you say, "I'm a millionaire" while drowning in debt, your brain will reject it as a lie.

How to Make Affirmations Work:

- **Be Specific**: Instead of "I'm successful," say, "I'm building a thriving career I'm proud of."
- **Focus on Progress**: Use affirmations like "I'm becoming more confident every day."
- **Tie Them to Action**: Pair affirmations with small, tangible steps.

Lessons from Elite Performers: Resilience and Grit

Elite athletes, entrepreneurs, and leaders don't succeed because they avoid challenges—they succeed because they embrace them. Resilience and grit are the twin pillars of mental armor, and here's what you can learn from the best:

1. The Growth Mindset

Elite performers view challenges as opportunities to grow. Instead of saying, "I can't do this," they say, "I can't do this yet."

2. The Power of Routine

Resilient people rely on habits to stay grounded. Morning rituals, exercise, and consistent sleep schedules create stability in chaotic environments.

3. Failing Forward

Grit isn't about avoiding failure—it's about learning from it. Every setback is a stepping stone. Elite performers don't see failure as the end; they see it as feedback.

Building Resilience: The Core of Mental Armor

Resilience is your ability to bounce back after setbacks. It's not something you're born with—it's something you cultivate. Here's how:

1. Reframe Failure

Instead of seeing failure as a reflection of your worth, see it as part of the process. Ask yourself:

- "What did I learn?"
- "How can I improve?"

2. Develop Emotional Agility

Emotional agility is the ability to navigate difficult emotions without being overwhelmed by them. Practice these steps:

- **Acknowledge**: Name your emotions without judgment.
- **Accept**: Allow yourself to feel without suppressing.
- **Act**: Choose constructive responses based on your

values.

3. Lean on Your Support System

Resilience isn't a solo journey. Build a network of supportive people who encourage and challenge you.

Exercises: Crafting Personalized Affirmations

This exercise will help you create affirmations tailored to your goals and challenges.

Step 1: Identify a Limiting Belief

Write down one belief that holds you back. For example: "I'm not smart enough to succeed."

Step 2: Flip the Script

Transform the belief into a positive statement. For example: "I am capable of learning and growing."

Step 3: Add Specificity

Make the affirmation actionable and relatable. For example: "I am learning new skills every day that bring me closer to success."

Step 4: Practice Daily

Repeat your affirmations aloud each morning or write them down in a journal.

Exercises: Perform a Resilience Audit

This exercise helps you assess your current resilience and identify areas for growth.

Step 1: Reflect on Past Challenges

Write down three times you overcame a difficult situation. For each, ask:

- What did I learn about myself?
- What strengths helped me get through it?

Step 2: Identify Weak Spots

Think about situations where you tend to struggle. For example:

- "I shut down when I receive criticism."
- "I avoid challenges because I fear failure."

Step 3: Create a Resilience Plan

For each weak spot, write down one action to strengthen your resilience. For example:

- Weak Spot: "I avoid challenges."
- Action: "I'll tackle one small challenge this week and reflect on the outcome."

Your Mental Armor Blueprint

By now, you've learned that mental armor isn't something you're born with—it's something you build. Through mindfulness, affirmations, and resilience, you can face life's challenges with strength and clarity.

This isn't about becoming unshakable—it's about learning to bend without breaking. The stronger your mental armor, the more unstoppable you become.

Part III: Becoming Unstoppable

Chapter 7: Break Free from Analysis Paralysis

The Trap of Overthinking

You know the feeling. You're standing at a crossroads, staring at the options, weighing every possible outcome. You tell yourself you just need more time to decide, but the truth is, you're stuck. The more you think, the harder it gets to move forward. This is the quicksand of analysis paralysis.

Analysis paralysis isn't a sign of intelligence or caution—it's a roadblock. It disguises itself as thoughtful deliberation, but its real purpose is to keep you from taking action. The more you overthink, the more overwhelmed you become, until even the simplest decisions feel impossible.

The good news? You don't have to stay stuck. Breaking free from analysis paralysis isn't about knowing the "right" answer—it's about learning to act despite uncertainty.

Why Overthinking Leads to Inaction

Overthinking is a self-sabotaging loop fueled by fear and perfectionism. Here's how it works:

1. **Fear of Failure**
   "What if I make the wrong choice?" This fear freezes you in place, convincing you that inaction is safer than risking a mistake.

2. **The Illusion of Control**

   Overthinking gives you the false sense that if you just analyze enough, you'll find the perfect solution. But perfection doesn't exist, and the quest for it keeps you stuck.

3. **Mental Exhaustion**

   The human brain can only process so much information before it shuts down. When you overanalyze, you drain your mental energy, making it even harder to decide.

The Cost of Inaction

Every time you hesitate, you lose time, opportunities, and momentum. The longer you stay in analysis paralysis, the harder it becomes to take that first step. Here's the reality:

- **Opportunities Expire**: Life doesn't wait for you to decide.
- **Regret Builds**: Inaction often leads to more regret than imperfect action.
- **Confidence Erodes**: The more you avoid decisions, the more you doubt your ability to make them.

The cost of overthinking isn't just external—it's internal. It chips away at your belief in yourself.

The "Just Start" Principle

Breaking free from analysis paralysis doesn't require perfect clarity—it requires movement. The "just start" principle is simple: take the smallest possible step forward.

Here's why it works:

- **Action Creates Clarity**: The act of doing often reveals answers you couldn't see while thinking.
- **Momentum Builds Motivation**: Each small step fuels the next, turning hesitation into progress.

Examples of Small, Messy Steps:

- Instead of planning a full workout routine, go for a 10-minute walk.
- Instead of writing a perfect report, jot down a rough outline.
- Instead of preparing for hours, start the conversation you've been dreading.

The goal isn't perfection—it's progress.

Decision-Making Hacks

If you're overwhelmed by choices, these decision-making tools can help:

1. The Two-Minute Rule

If a decision takes less than two minutes to make or execute, do it immediately. This clears small tasks from your mental load, leaving you with more energy for bigger decisions.

Example:

- Decision: Should I respond to this email now or later?
- Action: Respond immediately—it'll take less than two

minutes.

2. The 80/20 Principle (Pareto Principle)

Focus on the 20% of tasks or decisions that create 80% of your results.

Example:

- If you're overwhelmed by a to-do list, identify the one or two tasks that will make the biggest impact. Prioritize those, and let the rest wait.

3. The "Good Enough" Standard

Instead of aiming for the perfect choice, ask yourself, "What's good enough for now?" This shifts your focus from perfection to practicality.

The Courage to Decide

Making decisions isn't about always getting it right—it's about trusting yourself to handle the outcome. Even the wrong choice teaches you something valuable. The key is to act, learn, and adjust.

3 Questions to Simplify Decisions:

1. What's the worst that could happen?
2. What's the best that could happen?
3. What's the most likely outcome?

Exercise: Create a Decision Tree

This exercise helps you simplify overwhelming choices by mapping out your options and their potential outcomes.

Step 1: Identify the Decision

Write down a choice you're struggling with. For example: "Should I take a new job or stay in my current one?"

Step 2: List the Options

Underneath the decision, write down all possible actions. For example:

- Option 1: Accept the new job.
- Option 2: Stay in the current job.
- Option 3: Negotiate for better terms at the current job.

Step 3: Map the Outcomes

For each option, write down the best-case, worst-case, and most likely scenarios.

Step 4: Evaluate and Act

Look at your decision tree and ask yourself:

- Which option aligns with my values?
- Which outcome feels most manageable?
- What step can I take today to move forward?

Rewiring Your Mindset Around Decisions

Breaking free from analysis paralysis isn't just about tools and techniques—it's about changing the way you think about decisions.

Mindset Shifts to Embrace:

1. **There Are No Perfect Choices**: Every option has trade-offs. Progress matters more than precision.
2. **Mistakes Are Learning Opportunities**: Every wrong choice brings you closer to the right one.
3. **Small Steps Lead to Big Wins**: Action, no matter how small, is always better than inaction.

Your Decision-Making Blueprint

By the end of this chapter, you'll have the tools to break free from analysis paralysis and make decisions with confidence. Remember: the goal isn't to eliminate uncertainty—it's to move forward despite it.

The path to success isn't paved with perfect decisions. It's built with messy, imperfect steps. So stop overthinking, trust yourself, and take the leap.

Chapter 8: The Momentum Equation

The Power of Momentum

Success isn't born in a single leap. It's built step by step, win by win, in moments that compound over time. This is the power of momentum. Think of momentum as the invisible force that turns effort into acceleration. When you take consistent, intentional actions, momentum grows, making each step easier than the last.

Momentum is the difference between starting over and staying in motion. It's what turns small victories into transformative achievements. And the best part? Anyone can harness it.

Why Small Wins Matter

Big goals often feel overwhelming, but small wins provide the fuel to keep you moving. Here's why they're so powerful:

1. **Psychological Boost**
   Every time you achieve a small goal, your brain releases dopamine, the chemical of motivation and reward. This creates a positive feedback loop, reinforcing the desire to keep going.
2. **Proof of Progress**
   Small wins show you that change is possible. They build evidence that you're capable, which strengthens your confidence.
3. **Breaking Barriers**

Big goals can feel paralyzing. Small wins break them into manageable pieces, making progress achievable.

Example:

- Big Goal: Run a marathon.
- Small Wins: Start by running one mile, then two, then five. Each step builds confidence and strength.

The Compounding Effect of Small Wins

Momentum is like compounding interest: the more you invest, the faster it grows. Consider this:

- If you improve by just 1% every day, you'll be 37 times better by the end of the year.
- Small, consistent actions create exponential growth over time.

Real-World Example:

James Clear, author of *Atomic Habits*, shares the story of a coach who focused on helping his team improve by just 1% in various areas. The team didn't make dramatic changes overnight, but those small improvements compounded, leading them to become one of the most successful teams in history.

Momentum-Building Habits

Momentum doesn't rely on intensity—it relies on consistency. Here's how to build habits that keep you moving forward:

1. Start Tiny

Big changes are intimidating. Tiny actions are doable. Start so small that it's impossible to fail.

- Want to read more? Start with one page a day.
- Want to exercise? Do one push-up.

2. Focus on Consistency

It's better to do a little every day than a lot once in a while. Consistency builds trust in yourself.

3. Track Your Progress

Seeing your efforts add up is incredibly motivating. Use a journal, app, or tracker to record your wins.

4. Celebrate Every Victory

Don't wait for the big milestone to celebrate. Every step forward deserves recognition.

Real-World Examples of Momentum in Action

1. Sarah's Career Turnaround

Sarah was stuck in a dead-end job, unsure of how to move forward. Instead of overhauling her entire career, she started small: updating her resume, networking on LinkedIn, and applying to one job per week. Within six months, she landed her dream role.

2. Jake's Fitness Journey

Jake wanted to lose 50 pounds but struggled with motivation. Instead of focusing on the daunting number, he started walking 10 minutes a day. Gradually, he added more time and began eating healthier. A year later, Jake hit his goal and felt stronger than ever.

3. Maya's Financial Freedom

Maya was drowning in debt. She started by tracking her spending and cutting one unnecessary expense per week. Over time, she paid off her smallest debt, then the next. Today, she's debt-free and saving for her future.

The Momentum Equation

The Momentum Equation is simple:

Small Wins + Consistency + Time = Big Results

Each small win builds on the last, creating a snowball effect that transforms your efforts into unstoppable momentum.

Exercise: Start Your Momentum Tracker

This exercise helps you build and maintain momentum by tracking your daily wins.

Step 1: Choose an Area of Focus

Pick one area where you want to build momentum. For example:

- Health
- Career
- Relationships

Step 2: Set a Tiny Daily Goal

Identify one small, achievable action you can take each day. For example:

- Health: Drink one glass of water in the morning.
- Career: Write down one professional goal.
- Relationships: Send one kind message to a friend or loved one.

Step 3: Track Your Wins

Use a notebook, app, or calendar to record your daily actions. Create a simple system, like checking off a box or jotting down a quick note.

Step 4: Reflect Weekly

At the end of each week, review your tracker. Notice your progress and celebrate your consistency.

Overcoming Momentum Killers

Momentum can be fragile. Here's how to protect it:

1. Avoid Perfectionism

Missed a day? That's okay. Momentum isn't about perfection—it's about persistence. Get back on track the next day.

2. Limit Distractions

58

Identify and minimize anything that pulls you away from your goals.

3. Stay Flexible

Life happens. Adjust your actions as needed, but don't stop moving.

Your Momentum Blueprint

By now, you understand that momentum isn't about massive leaps—it's about consistent, intentional steps. It's the small wins, compounded over time, that lead to big achievements.

Start today. Choose one area, take one step, and let the momentum carry you forward. Because once you get moving, nothing can stop you.

Chapter 9: The Conquer Anything Toolkit

Your Arsenal for Action

Life throws obstacles at all of us—fear, procrastination, and overwhelm are universal challenges. The difference between those who thrive and those who falter isn't the absence of these barriers—it's the tools they use to break through them.

This chapter is your personalized toolkit. It's packed with strategies to conquer fear, silence procrastination, and manage overwhelm, so you can move forward with clarity and purpose. You don't need to wait for the "right time" or "perfect conditions." With the right tools, you can take action today.

Overcoming Fear: Your First Tool

Fear's Real Role

Fear isn't your enemy. It's a signal. It tells you you're stepping into unfamiliar territory, which often means growth. The problem isn't fear itself—it's how you respond to it.

Reframe Fear as Excitement

Your body doesn't know the difference between fear and excitement—it processes both as heightened energy. The next time fear rises, tell yourself, "I'm excited to try this." This simple shift rewires your perspective.

Face It in Pieces

Fear often feels overwhelming because you're looking at the whole picture. Break it down:

- What's the worst-case scenario?
- How likely is it to happen?
- What's one small step you can take to test the waters?

Silencing Procrastination: Your Second Tool

Why We Procrastinate

Procrastination isn't laziness—it's avoidance. We put things off because they feel too big, too hard, or too uncertain.

Tools to Overcome Procrastination:

1. **The Two-Minute Rule**
   If a task takes less than two minutes, do it immediately. For longer tasks, commit to just two minutes of effort to get started. Momentum often follows.
2. **The Timer Technique**
   Set a timer for 25 minutes (Pomodoro technique) and work on your task without distractions. When the timer ends, take a five-minute break.
3. **Reward Yourself**
   Pair tasks with rewards. For example, "I'll watch my favorite show after I finish this report."

Managing Overwhelm: Your Third Tool

The Mindset Shift

Overwhelm happens when we focus on everything at once. Shift your mindset: you don't have to do everything—you just have to do the next thing.

The Prioritization Framework:

1. **Brain Dump**
   Write down everything on your mind. Getting it out of your head reduces mental clutter.
2. **Categorize Tasks**
   Use the Eisenhower Matrix:
   - Urgent & Important: Do now.
   - Important but Not Urgent: Schedule it.
   - Urgent but Not Important: Delegate it.
   - Neither Urgent Nor Important: Eliminate it.
3. **Take One Small Step**
   Choose the most critical task and break it into smaller pieces. Focus only on the first step.

Visualization Techniques: Mentally Rehearsing Success

Why Visualization Works

Your brain can't distinguish between vividly imagined experiences and real ones. Visualization creates a mental blueprint, helping you feel more prepared and confident.

How to Visualize Effectively:

1. **Set the Scene**

Close your eyes and imagine yourself achieving your goal. Engage all your senses: What do you see, hear, feel, smell, and taste?

2. **Focus on the Process**

   Don't just picture the outcome—visualize the steps you'll take to get there.

3. **Rehearse Daily**

   Spend 5–10 minutes each day visualizing your success. This consistency strengthens your mental pathways.

Goal-Setting Frameworks: SMART Goals and Vision Boards

SMART Goals

SMART goals are Specific, Measurable, Achievable, Relevant, and Time-bound.

How to Create SMART Goals:

1. **Specific**: Define exactly what you want to achieve.
   - Instead of: "Get in shape."
   - Say: "Lose 10 pounds in 3 months by exercising 4 times a week."
2. **Measurable**: Include criteria to track progress.
   - Example: "I'll track my workouts and meals in an app."
3. **Achievable**: Make it realistic based on your resources.
4. **Relevant**: Ensure the goal aligns with your bigger vision.
5. **Time-Bound**: Set a deadline to create urgency.

Vision Boards

Vision boards are powerful tools for clarifying and focusing on your goals.

How to Create a Vision Board:

1. **Gather Supplies**: Use a board, magazines, or a digital platform like Pinterest.
2. **Define Your Goals**: Write down what you want to achieve in different areas of life (health, career, relationships).
3. **Choose Inspiring Images**: Select pictures, quotes, and symbols that represent your goals.
4. **Place It Somewhere Visible**: Keep your vision board where you'll see it daily as a reminder of your aspirations.

Exercises: Create Your "Conquer Anything" Action Plan

This exercise will help you combine the tools in this chapter into a personalized plan for overcoming obstacles and achieving your goals.

Step 1: Identify Your Goal

Write down one specific goal you want to achieve. For example: "I want to start my own business within six months."

Step 2: Break It Down

64

List the steps required to achieve your goal. Break each step into smaller, actionable tasks.

Step 3: Apply the Tools

- **Fear**: Identify what scares you about this goal. Use reframing techniques to turn fear into excitement.
- **Procrastination**: Use the two-minute rule or timer technique to start your tasks.
- **Overwhelm**: Brain dump all related tasks and prioritize them.

Step 4: Visualize Success

Spend 5 minutes visualizing yourself achieving this goal. Picture the steps and the final outcome.

Step 5: Track Progress

Create a simple tracker (journal, app, or spreadsheet) to monitor your daily actions and wins.

Real-Life Applications

The tools in this chapter have transformed countless lives. Here are a few examples:

1. Overcoming Fear

Emma used visualization to prepare for her first public speaking event. By rehearsing success in her mind, she felt confident and delivered a powerful talk.

2. Battling Procrastination

Jake started using the two-minute rule to tackle his writing projects. What once felt daunting became manageable, and he completed his book within a year.

3. Managing Overwhelm

Maya created a vision board to clarify her priorities. By focusing on what truly mattered, she eliminated distractions and built a thriving business.

Your Conquer Anything Blueprint

By now, you've built a toolkit to overcome fear, procrastination, and overwhelm. You've learned how to visualize success, set effective goals, and create actionable plans.

Remember, the tools are only as powerful as your willingness to use them. Start today. Choose one tool, take one step, and watch as you conquer anything in your path.

Part IV: Living the Unstoppable Life

Chapter 10: Resilience: The True Superpower

Why Resilience Matters

Resilience is the invisible force that keeps you moving forward when life knocks you down. It's not about avoiding failure or setbacks—it's about bouncing back stronger every time you fall. Resilience transforms obstacles into opportunities and challenges into stepping stones.

If confidence is the engine that drives you forward, resilience is the fuel that keeps the engine running no matter the terrain. Without it, even the most talented and ambitious people crumble under pressure. But with resilience, you become unstoppable.

This chapter is your guide to building the kind of resilience that can weather any storm.

What Is Resilience?

Resilience isn't toughness—it's adaptability. It's the ability to bend without breaking, to recover when things don't go as planned. Resilient people don't avoid adversity; they embrace it as part of the process.

Think of resilience as a muscle. The more you exercise it, the stronger it becomes. And just like any other skill, resilience can be learned and cultivated.

Bouncing Back from Failures and Setbacks

Failure Is a Teacher, Not a Verdict

Society often frames failure as something to avoid at all costs. But failure is simply feedback. It's a way of learning what doesn't work, so you can get closer to what does.

Consider this:

- Thomas Edison failed over 1,000 times before inventing the light bulb.
- J.K. Rowling was rejected by 12 publishers before *Harry Potter* found a home.

These people weren't immune to failure—they were resilient in the face of it.

The Bounce-Back Process

1. **Acknowledge the Setback**
   Don't ignore or minimize what happened. Name it, understand it, and own it.
2. **Reframe the Experience**
   Instead of asking, "Why did this happen to me?" ask, "What can I learn from this?"
3. **Take the Next Step**
   Resilience isn't about solving everything at once—it's about taking one small action to move forward.

Building Resilience Through Adversity

Adversity isn't something to fear—it's something to embrace. Every challenge you face is an opportunity to grow stronger and more capable.

Lessons Adversity Teaches

1. **Perspective**
   Difficult times remind you of what truly matters. They strip away distractions and focus your energy on what's important.
2. **Resourcefulness**
   When faced with limited options, you learn to think creatively and find solutions you never would have considered.
3. **Inner Strength**
   Adversity reveals your capacity to endure and overcome.

Examples of Resilience in Action

- **Nelson Mandela** endured 27 years in prison and emerged not with bitterness, but with a commitment to reconciliation and leadership.
- **Oprah Winfrey** overcame poverty, abuse, and rejection to become one of the most influential figures in the world.

The Resilience Framework

Resilience isn't about ignoring pain or pretending everything is fine—it's about processing, adapting, and thriving.

1. Emotional Regulation

Learn to manage your emotions, so they don't overwhelm you.

- Practice mindfulness to stay grounded.
- Journaling can help you process your feelings and gain clarity.

2. Self-Efficacy

Believe in your ability to influence outcomes.

- Reflect on past successes, no matter how small.
- Set achievable goals to reinforce your sense of capability.

3. Social Support

Resilience isn't a solo journey. Surround yourself with people who encourage and uplift you.

- Share your struggles with trusted friends or mentors.
- Seek out communities that align with your values.

4. Optimism

Cultivate a mindset that focuses on possibilities rather than problems.

- Practice gratitude daily by listing three things you're thankful for.
- Challenge negative thoughts with evidence of past triumphs.

Why Resilience Makes You Truly Unstoppable

The Resilience Advantage

Resilient people don't avoid challenges—they embrace them. They understand that failure and setbacks are inevitable on the path to success. But instead of seeing these moments as the end, they see them as the beginning of something new.

The Compounding Effect of Resilience

Every time you bounce back, you reinforce your belief in your own strength. This compounding effect makes you more willing to take risks, pursue big goals, and face uncertainty head-on.

Exercises for Building Resilience

1. Write Your Resilience Story

Reflect on a time when you faced adversity and overcame it.

- What was the challenge?
- How did you respond?
- What did you learn about yourself?

Writing your story reminds you of your strength and prepares you for future challenges.

2. Create a Resilience Toolkit

Identify tools and practices that help you stay grounded and recover quickly. For example:

- Deep breathing exercises

- Inspirational quotes or books
- A list of supportive friends to call

3. Practice a Daily Resilience Ritual

Develop a habit that reinforces your resilience, such as:

- Journaling about one challenge and how you'll tackle it.
- Meditating for 10 minutes to center yourself.

The Power of a Resilient Mindset

Resilience isn't just about surviving—it's about thriving. It's the foundation of confidence, adaptability, and unstoppable progress.

When you build resilience, you don't just prepare for challenges—you welcome them as opportunities to grow. You don't just endure setbacks—you use them as stepping stones to something greater.

Your Resilience Blueprint

By the end of this chapter, you'll have the tools to cultivate unshakable resilience. Remember: resilience isn't the absence of struggle—it's the ability to move through it with grace and determination.

Your journey will have highs and lows, but with resilience, you'll never be stopped. You'll bend, but you won't break. And every time you rise, you'll rise stronger.

Chapter 11: The Unstoppable Mindset

What It Means to Be Truly Unstoppable

Being unstoppable isn't about never facing challenges—it's about meeting them with confidence and grace. It's about knowing that no matter what life throws your way, you'll find a way to adapt, grow, and thrive. The unstoppable mindset isn't a destination—it's a journey.

This chapter will show you how to cultivate that mindset for life. You'll learn how to maintain your momentum, stay confident, and embrace uncertainty as an ally, not an enemy.

The Foundation of Lifelong Growth

Growth Is a Lifelong Commitment

Growth isn't a one-time event—it's a continuous process. The unstoppable mindset thrives on curiosity, adaptability, and a willingness to evolve.

Why Growth Fuels Confidence

Confidence and growth are deeply connected. The more you learn and improve, the more capable you feel. Every new skill or insight reinforces your belief in your ability to navigate the world.

Habits and Systems for Maintaining Momentum

Momentum isn't self-sustaining—it requires intentional effort. The habits and systems you build are the scaffolding that supports your unstoppable mindset.

1. Focus on Daily Wins

Momentum is built one day at a time. Start each day by setting small, achievable goals, and end each day by reflecting on your progress.

2. Create Non-Negotiable Habits

Anchor your day with habits that align with your values and goals. For example:

- Morning: Journaling or mindfulness practice to set your intention.
- Evening: A gratitude journal to reinforce positivity.

3. Build Feedback Loops

Feedback loops help you stay on track and make adjustments.

- Weekly Review: Assess what worked, what didn't, and what you'll improve.
- Monthly Goals: Set clear, measurable objectives for the month ahead.

4. Stay Consistent, Not Perfect

Progress matters more than perfection. Missed a day? That's okay—get back on track without guilt.

The Role of Systems Over Willpower

Willpower is finite. Systems are sustainable. Here's how to design systems that keep you moving forward:

1. Automate Decisions

Reduce decision fatigue by creating routines. For example:

- Meal prep on Sundays to simplify weekday meals.
- Schedule workouts at the same time each week.

2. Use Accountability

Share your goals with a trusted friend, coach, or community. Accountability keeps you motivated and aligned with your intentions.

3. Reward Consistency

Celebrate your efforts, not just your results. Rewards reinforce habits and make the process enjoyable.

Confidence That Stands the Test of Time

Confidence isn't about knowing everything—it's about trusting yourself to figure things out. The unstoppable mindset builds confidence that lasts by focusing on adaptability and resilience.

1. Confidence Through Competence

The more you do, the more you grow. Confidence isn't a feeling—it's the result of action.

2. Confidence Through Self-Talk

Positive, constructive self-talk reinforces your belief in your abilities. When doubts arise, counter them with affirmations or logical responses.

3. Confidence Through Failure

Every failure is an opportunity to learn and grow. Reframe mistakes as stepping stones, not roadblocks.

Embracing Uncertainty as Part of Your Journey

Why We Fear Uncertainty

Uncertainty feels uncomfortable because it's unpredictable. The human brain craves stability and control, so when the future is unclear, fear and doubt creep in.

The Gift of Uncertainty

Uncertainty isn't your enemy—it's your ally. It means you're stepping into the unknown, where growth happens. When you embrace uncertainty, you open yourself to possibilities you couldn't have imagined.

How to Embrace Uncertainty

1. **Reframe the Unknown**
   Instead of seeing uncertainty as chaos, view it as an adventure. Ask yourself: "What exciting opportunities might this bring?"
2. **Focus on What You Can Control**
   You can't control the outcome, but you can control your actions. Focus on taking the next step, no matter how

small.

3. **Trust the Process**

   Growth isn't linear. Trust that every step, even the uncertain ones, is leading you in the right direction.

Exercises to Cultivate the Unstoppable Mindset

1. The Confidence Log

Keep a journal where you document:

- Challenges you've faced and overcome.
- Skills you've learned.
- Wins, big or small.

Reflecting on your progress reinforces your belief in your abilities.

2. The Growth Contract

Write a contract with yourself that commits to lifelong growth. Include statements like:

- "I will embrace challenges as opportunities to grow."
- "I will prioritize progress over perfection."
- "I will trust myself to navigate uncertainty."

Review this contract whenever doubts arise.

3. The Uncertainty Practice

Identify one area in your life where uncertainty holds you back.

- Take one small, courageous step into the unknown.
- Reflect on what you learned and how it felt.

Over time, this practice builds your tolerance for uncertainty.

Real-World Stories of the Unstoppable Mindset

1. Rachel's Career Pivot

Rachel worked in a stable but unfulfilling job. Embracing uncertainty, she enrolled in a coding bootcamp, even though it meant stepping into the unknown. Today, she's thriving in a career she loves.

2. Tom's Fitness Transformation

Tom struggled with consistency. By focusing on small daily wins and celebrating progress, he built momentum that led to lasting change.

3. Priya's Entrepreneurial Journey

Priya launched her business in the face of doubt and uncertainty. By trusting the process and leaning on her support system, she turned her vision into reality.

The Unstoppable Blueprint

By now, you've learned that the unstoppable mindset is about more than confidence—it's about action, adaptability, and resilience.

To stay unstoppable:

1. Commit to daily growth.
2. Build systems that support your momentum.
3. Embrace uncertainty as a natural and necessary part of the journey.

Your path won't always be clear, but with the unstoppable mindset, you'll have the tools to navigate it. Keep moving forward, and trust that you're capable of achieving extraordinary things.

Chapter 12: Passing It On

Why Transformation is Meant to Be Shared

Your journey to becoming unstoppable doesn't end with you—it begins with how you inspire others. True transformation is contagious. The confidence, courage, and momentum you've built have the power to ripple outward, impacting everyone you touch.

When you share your story, mentor others, or lead by example, you create a legacy of action and courage. You show others what's possible, even when they doubt themselves. And here's the beautiful twist: by helping others, you strengthen your own transformation.

This chapter is about stepping into that role, using your growth to uplift others, and leaving a legacy that lasts far beyond your lifetime.

Inspiring Others Through Your Transformation

Why Your Story Matters

You might think, "Who am I to inspire others?" But your story is your greatest asset. It's not about being perfect—it's about being real. People don't connect with perfection; they connect with authenticity.

Your struggles, triumphs, and lessons learned are a roadmap for others. By sharing them, you show people that transformation is possible for them too.

How to Inspire Others

1. **Lead by Example**
   People learn more from what you do than what you say. Live your values, and others will naturally follow.
2. **Share Your Journey**
   Be open about your challenges and how you overcame them. Whether it's through conversation, social media, or writing, your story can spark change.
3. **Celebrate Others' Wins**
   Acknowledge and celebrate the progress of those around you. Your encouragement can be the spark someone needs to keep going.

Helping Others Strengthens Your Confidence

The Confidence-Boosting Power of Helping Others

When you help others, you reinforce your own growth. Here's why:

- Teaching solidifies your knowledge and skills.
- Seeing someone else succeed because of your guidance affirms your impact.
- Encouraging others reminds you of your own resilience and capabilities.

Ways to Help Others

1. **Mentorship**
   Offer guidance to someone who's just starting their journey. You don't have to be an expert—you just need to be one step ahead.
2. **Acts of Service**
   Helping doesn't always require words. Small acts of kindness—listening, supporting, or lending a hand—can have a profound impact.
3. **Community Involvement**
   Join or create groups where people can grow together. Sharing ideas and experiences in a collective space multiplies their impact.

Leaving a Legacy of Action and Courage

What Is a Legacy?

Your legacy isn't about fame or recognition—it's about the lives you touch. It's the example you set, the values you embody, and the impact you leave behind.

How to Build Your Legacy

1. **Define Your Core Values**
   Ask yourself: What do I want to be remembered for? Write down the principles that matter most to you.
2. **Live Intentionally**
   Align your actions with your values. Consistency builds trust and inspires others.

3. **Create Opportunities for Others**
   Use your resources, knowledge, and influence to open doors for others.

The Ripple Effect of Courage

When you act with courage, you give others permission to do the same. Your bravery becomes a lighthouse, guiding others through their own storms.

Real-Life Examples of Leaving a Legacy

1. **Malala Yousafzai**
   Despite facing unimaginable challenges, Malala's courage inspired a global movement for girls' education. Her story shows the ripple effect of standing for what you believe in.
2. **Mister Rogers**
   Fred Rogers didn't just teach kindness—he lived it. His legacy of compassion continues to inspire millions.
3. **Your Story**
   You don't have to be famous to leave a legacy. Every act of courage, every life you touch, adds to the ripple effect of your transformation.

Exercises for Passing It On

1. Write Your Legacy Statement

Take time to reflect on the impact you want to leave behind. Write a statement that captures your values, purpose, and vision for the future.

Example:

"I want to be remembered as someone who empowered others to believe in themselves, take action, and create meaningful change in their lives."

2. Mentor Someone

Identify one person you can mentor. Share your story, offer guidance, and celebrate their progress.

3. Create a Gratitude Circle

Gather a group of friends, family, or colleagues. Take turns sharing what you're grateful for and what inspires you. This practice reinforces positivity and connection.

Your Role as a Ripple Maker

Transformation doesn't stop with you—it expands through you. By sharing your story, helping others, and living with courage, you create ripples of change that extend far beyond what you can see.

Your legacy isn't defined by a single moment. It's built every day, in every interaction, and in every life you touch.

The Power of Collective Growth

Imagine a world where everyone commits to lifting each other up. Every person who embraces their potential inspires others to do the same. This is the collective power of transformation, and it starts with you.

By passing it on, you're not just building your legacy—you're contributing to a movement of courage, confidence, and unstoppable momentum.

Your Legacy Blueprint

By the end of this chapter, you'll have the tools to inspire others, strengthen your confidence through service, and leave a legacy that matters. Remember: your transformation isn't just for you—it's a gift to the world.

So, take what you've learned, live it boldly, and share it generously. Because when you pass it on, you don't just change lives—you change the world.

Conclusion: Your First Step

The Journey Begins with a Single Step

Every great achievement starts with a single step forward. Every transformation begins with a moment of decision. This is your moment. You've reached the end of this book, but the beginning of your journey.

The tools, strategies, and insights you've gained are powerful, but they're only as effective as your willingness to use them. Progress doesn't come from knowing—it comes from doing. Imperfect action, even if it feels small or uncertain, is the only way forward.

Why Imperfect Action is the Key

We often wait for the "perfect moment" to begin, telling ourselves that when we're more confident, more prepared, or more ready, we'll act. But here's the truth: perfection is a myth. The perfect time doesn't exist, and waiting for it only delays your growth.

Imperfect Action Builds Momentum

- When you take even the smallest step, you create momentum. Each action, no matter how imperfect, moves you closer to your goals.

Imperfect Action Builds Confidence

- Confidence isn't the prerequisite for action—it's the

result. Every time you take a step, you prove to yourself that you're capable.

Why Today Matters

There's no better time to start than now. The future isn't promised, and the only thing you truly control is this moment. Starting today, however imperfectly, sends a powerful message to yourself:

"I am ready to grow. I am ready to change. I am ready to take the first step toward becoming unstoppable."

Your First Steps Toward Transformation

Here's how to take that first step:

1. Choose One Action

You don't have to tackle everything at once. Choose one small, meaningful action that aligns with your goals.

Example:

- If your goal is to build confidence, say "yes" to one opportunity today that challenges you.
- If your goal is to overcome procrastination, spend two minutes working on a task you've been avoiding.

2. Commit to Progress Over Perfection

Tell yourself, "Done is better than perfect." Celebrate the fact that you started, even if it's messy.

3. Reflect and Adjust

After taking your first step, reflect on what you learned. What worked? What didn't? Use those insights to refine your approach moving forward.

A Journey, Not a Destination

Becoming unstoppable isn't about reaching a final destination—it's about committing to the journey. There will be challenges, setbacks, and moments of doubt. But there will also be growth, triumph, and moments of clarity that make every step worthwhile.

Your Journey Will Include:

- **Growth**: You'll discover strengths you never knew you had.
- **Learning**: Every mistake will teach you something valuable.
- **Resilience**: You'll bounce back stronger from every setback.

Your Future Self is Waiting

Picture the version of yourself who has embraced the unstoppable mindset. What do they look like? How do they move through the world? What have they achieved?

That future self is waiting for you. Every step you take brings you closer to them. And the only way to get there is to start walking.

Exercise: Your First Step Action Plan

Step 1: Identify Your Goal

Write down one goal you want to work toward.

Step 2: Break It Down

List the smallest, simplest step you can take today to move closer to that goal.

Step 3: Take Action

Commit to completing that step today, no matter how imperfectly.

Step 4: Reflect and Celebrate

At the end of the day, write down what you accomplished and how it felt to take action.

A Final Reminder

The journey to becoming unstoppable doesn't require perfection. It requires courage, consistency, and the willingness to keep going, even when the path is unclear.

Your transformation begins not when you're ready, but when you decide. That decision, made today, is the first step toward the life you've imagined.

A Motivational Call to Action

The world is waiting for you to step into your potential. It's waiting for your ideas, your voice, and your courage. Don't let fear or doubt hold you back.

You've read the words. You've gained the tools. Now it's time to act.

Stand up. Take that first step. And remember: you are unstoppable.